Garden*home*|C I T Y

Garden*home*|CITY

Creating an Urban Haven

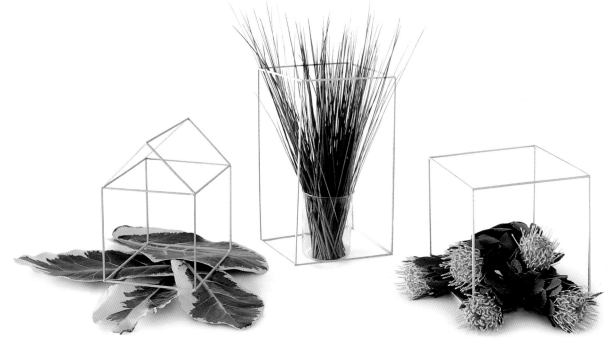

BY BONNIE TRUST DAHAN

PHOTOGRAPHS BY SEAN SULLIVAN

STYLING BY ANTHONY ALBERTUS

CHRONICLE BOOKS

SAN FRANCISCO

Library of Congress Cataloging-in-Publication Data: available.

ISBN: 0-8118-3247-3

Printed in China

Photographs by Shaun Sullivan

Styling by Anthony Albertus

Designed by Sandra McHenry Design

Distributed in Canada by

Raincoast Books

9050 Shaughnessy Street

Vancouver, British Columbia V6P 6E5

10 9 8 7 6 5 4 3 2 1

Chronicle Books LLC

85 Second Street

San Francisco, California 94105

www.chroniclebooks.com

Dedication

To Steve, an experienced gardener, who always encourages me to seek the light in order to grow.

Acknowledgments

Once again my supremely talented partners from the original *Garden House* design and photography team have made the evolution of this new book a joyful endeavor. Despite the extraordinary demands I placed on them, Shaun Sullivan, photographer extraordinaire, and Anthony Albertus, super stylist, continued to dazzle me with their interpretations of my vision. Aside from a few well-deserved jibes about my tendency to ask for more shots in one day than humanly possible, they responded with elan and creativity. Their artistry and commitment to perfection are evident in every photograph in this book. Sandra McHenry designed a brilliant format that served as the foundation for our photography and became a celebration of the details that define city garden style. Leslie Jonath's constant inspiration and unflagging devotion to the concept brought this book to life and helped it thrive through all stages of its evolution. Finally, I am deeply grateful to all of the generous people who opened their homes to us and invited us to experience their resourcefulness as urban garden artists.

CONTENTS

I N T R O D U C T I O N

City garden style is a state of mind that creates a sense of a garden where there is none. It requires only an instinct for color and an eye for composition, and perhaps an inclination toward a remembered scent. Instead of curtailing imaginative expression, viewing your home in the city through a garden filter can set you off in new and surprising directions. By looking for ways to use subtle or larger-than-life reminders in every room of an urban set-

Split-leaf philodendron stems make a strong statement in a glass vase and have more staying power than a floral bouquet.

ting, city garden style keeps you in touch with the delight, the healing powers, and the soul-satisfying beauty of the garden. ◗ As you will see here, whether you live in a modern high-rise, a loft, an older flat, or a house, bringing the outdoors in enhances any lifestyle. From contemporary to antique to country to ethnic, you can always find flowers, plants, natural materials, and garden icons that can transform your living space into a garden retreat. A small, sparsely furnished studio looking out onto a jumbled urbanscape shows its garden influence with an audacious display of dozens of tulips tumbling from a wide-mouthed vase layered with

Cabbage flowers contrast with dark, carved mango wood vases.

limes and kumquats. In a spacious loft, cabbages punctuate hundreds of tiny chrysanthemum heads to form a unique dining table runner. In an old flat, a kitchen brick wall acts as a contrasting backdrop for the potting-shed sensibility created by galvanized containers and a farmers' market bounty of citrus and roses. ◊ Whatever your personal taste may be, city life often demands that you express it succinctly. Limited space, architectural considerations, compressed time, and uneven light all play a role in the way you decorate. Out of necessity, city dwellers develop a more selective eye and become good editors. A few cut philodendron stems in a sleek glass container add graphic impact, while a single violet set afloat in a ceramic dish offers a cheery morning greeting. A simple lemon-colored hyacinth perched on a windowsill fills an empty room with its sweet, luscious fragrance. An outdoor plant that thrives indoors, a swing in the living room, or a wall color reminiscent of a particular flower can instantly transport you from the concrete pallor of the city to the Impressionist palette of Giverny, the vibrant colors of summer annuals, or a cherished memory of a childhood garden.

Each simple note resonates with the senses and engages the imagination. ◗ In the pages that follow, we see how ingenious garden lovers reinvented a wide range of spaces by using city garden style. While their ideas may have originated to solve a particular challenge or to enliven a specific environment, they can be easily adapted to all types of locations. Whether you have your own plot of land to glean from, or rely on a weekly farmers' market or the corner grocery, seeing these solutions at work in other contexts will spark ideas that will enable you to create your own variation on the garden theme. ◗ Essentially, in whatever form it takes, an urban garden home creates a world within a world. It's a personal nest—a haven that can nurture and bring peace of mind. Bringing a touch of the garden indoors helps enliven us at the end of a day. In any form, either elaborate or suggestive, painted in bold, vivid strokes or evocative, pastel washes, it is always a visual cocktail for the spirit. Surrounding ourselves with a garden retreat prompts us to pay attention to what truly matters and dissuades us from moving so fast we forget to stop, look, and listen. City garden style is a gentle reminder that sometimes we need to take our garden with us wherever we go. ◗

Floating pink cymbidium orchid heads in a flat bowl extends their life and gives the viewer a new perspective on this lush, tropical plant.

CITY HOUSE

Whether your house in the city is freestanding or attached to a row of other houses, it often has some access to the outdoors. These exterior spaces can vary from full gardens to small terraces or rooftops. No matter what their size or configuration, the spaces adjacent to a city house provide the potential that invites garden inspiration and offer you the opportunity to grow plants, flowers, and trees. ◖ Architectural styles in city houses vary with regional and neighborhood influences and offer the widest range of possibility for enhancement. They typically have more square footage and multiple light sources than apartments or flats. If you own your city home, you can make structural modifications such as adding skylights, atriums, or French doors. To take advantage of all the garden has to offer, you may decide to remove isolating barriers between exterior and interior living spaces by replacing small windows with larger ones that let in more light and offer full garden views. Or you can add a small terrace so the surrounding scenery is more accessible indoors. ◖

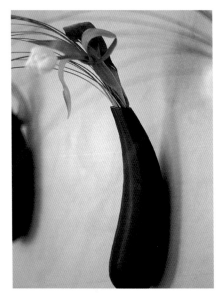

In this environmentally designed house, a wall of six organically shaped vases creates living art. The sage green and lavender natural pigments incorporated into the plaster of both walls were inspired by garden hues.

◖ Yet you can still bring the outside in without remodeling. By selectively foraging in the garden you can create artful arrangements of stones, branches, leaves, and flowers that mingle textures, shapes, and hues with the casual elegance of nature. In this way, city garden style keeps you more fully in touch with the seasons. As the seasons change, so do the choices of found objects and colors—bright greens in April, russets in October. A budding forsythia branch in early spring can be replaced by a lichen-covered bough in autumn. You may decide to extend a tropical vacation by assembling plants and flowers grown in your own backyard whose vivid tones and exotic leaf shapes bring back sun-filled memories.

◖ Contrast and juxtaposition are two decorative strategies available to city garden homes. In one room, a window that looks out onto a downtown skyline may also provide the backdrop for a slender glass vase holding a solitary flower stem. In another, contemporary furnishings play off the audacious fronds of a banana plant on a dining room table. The opportunities for creating a refuge that welcomes in the garden are plentiful in any urban dwelling, but flourish in the larger interior of a house whose expandable space can reach out to fulfill a yearning for the outdoors. ◖

This remarkable city house combines environmental architecture with a high design aesthetic. The owner wisely noted that the entrance is a place where guests tend to linger, so a dramatic poured-concrete wall piece was the solution. Three periwinkle lotuses gracefully dip over the outside edge of a fountain as water softly cascades over the ledge from a shallow pool.

Plant and building material choices in this light-filled living room reflect a true respect for resources and the possibilities of recycling. The fireplace bench, constructed of cast-in-place concrete, is embedded with turquoise and small stones and is etched with a lotus flower. Upended stair treads reclaimed from an old French schoolhouse form the front piece. Distressed green metal square vases hold quince and yellow twig dogwood branches. Succulents are planted in an old birdbath and sit atop antique scales. Able to withstand neglect and minimal watering, they make an excellent ecological choice for time-starved city dwellers.

Clipping the blooms of a tired orchid and floating them in a shallow bowl of water prolongs their life and offers a new way to admire their sensual beauty. A handful of yellow, orange, and red fritillaria in a petite wood vase plays off the vibrant colors found on this table. A collection of natural objects juxtaposed on a rolled reed runner illustrates that it only takes a little imagination to replace the conventional floral arrangement in a crystal vase with a more original alternative. Cocoa palm fiber husks lined with chartreuse baobab pods arc gracefully, lending energy to this unexpected arrangement.

The serene and restful ambience of this bedroom is in part created by the choice of wall color. Natural pigment skillfully blended into the plaster of the walls produces a soft watercolor effect that evokes visions of lavender fields or a Monet painting. The gentle perfumes of fresh lavender, jasmine, and daphne mingle to further encourage sweet dreams.

Following the ecological design principles used throughout this city house, a floor-to-ceiling window catches enough natural light to accommodate the needs of a potted palm tree. Pool moss helps keep the plant moist, and rocks mounded in the container keep dirt from splattering when the owner showers. Flooring made from recycled Alaskan cedar allows for drainage. Every opportunity to bring in a light touch of the garden has been taken. A recessed wall shelf intended for shampoo and soap presents Lenten roses in a dark stone vase. The concrete countertop features an embedded leaf coaster.

This playfully adorned dining table is positioned to take full advantage of both the sunny view and garden breezes coming in through doors thrown open onto a small patio. The imaginative combination of plant and decorative materials creates a fanciful theme at minimal cost. Huge banana leaves soar from lime green vases like otherworldly winged beings. A pineapple plant secured in a pot with pool moss continues the tropical fantasy. Organza leaves scattered on the yellow silk runner serve as coasters for lemons plucked from a nearby tree.

The niche carved into this bathroom wall
serves as a natural altar whose contents
rotate with the seasons. Round gourds
become vases for whole dried pears.
A sudden inspiration led to the scattering
of reddish purple Princess flower leaves.
Even in a dark area, a poetic touch of
nature has an uplifting effect.

A stalk of bamboo in a vase is eye-catching in the light on a shelf next to the shower. Another planted bamboo on the sink continues the naturalistic theme. Believed to bring good luck, bamboo stalks are often found sprouting in Asian homes.

The instinct to forage in a small city garden transcends season. Even in autumn, this urban gardener searched among fallen leaves and drying foliage with a selective eye toward unique and evocative shapes, colors, and textures. Collected outdoors on a weathered antique picnic table and displayed indoors in simple containers, stunning arrangements visually fuse the interior and exterior of this townhouse. Six speckled river stones gathered from the graveled garden floor are transformed into singular, meditative notes when showcased on small, footed celadon plates carefully spaced across a kitchen counter.

In this natural centerpiece created by glass containers in staggered sizes, chinaberry branches lean on a bed of stones in a wide-mouthed, round cylinder. Artfully arranged in a larger cylinder, lichen-covered oak branches pruned from the garden become natural sculpture. Mossy rocks piled in a round glass bowl complete the wood-land triptych.

Subtle variations of tone-on-tone green and gray define this autumnal city garden accentuated by scattered russet and gold leaves. Gradations of color and shape bring textural interest to the natural river-rock gravel. The eye is guided toward the focal point of two teak chairs and then upward to taller buildings in the distance—a reminder that the muted colors of this secret niche create a soothing retreat from the harsh edges of the city that surrounds it.

An antique trough on a weathered picnic table holds branches of delicate lime-colored chinaberries. The gray of the teak integrates with the soft sages and limes of the foliage while rays of sunlight etch leaf forms and highlight patterns on river-rock gravel. If you squint, it's not difficult to imagine this garden in June, as a twilight setting for a summer alfresco dinner.

S M A L L   A P A R T M E N T

I n a city apartment, it is easy to see how small touches can transform small spaces. With minimal access to the outdoors, juxtaposition to other nearby buildings, compromised light sources, and combined living areas, you must draw inspiration from the city itself. Creating a garden-style apartment amidst the buzz and hum of the city is essentially a process

Despite its compact size, this tiny sitting room reflects a strong connection to the garden. Horsetail in a celadon vase is echoed in a ladder mirror propped near a window that looks out on a red-leaved plum tree.

of carefully selecting and arranging a collection of small garden elements. How you select these components depends on the way you live. Whatever your situation, you can take advantage of the city's rich resources to add color, foliage, outdoor furniture, and ornament suited to your apartment's size and style, creating niches that can become miniature, nurturing havens. ❧ A garden-style apartment can also be a simple way to extend a small living space. You can blur the boundaries between indoors and out with the clever use of plants, containers, and other garden accessories that are unique to city environments, colonizing

window boxes, fire escapes, and balconies. A strategically placed mirror reflects a garden and transports it inside. Plinths, watering cans, and garden ladders from flea markets can serve as rustic containers and platforms for plants. On a table by the window, a small potted geranium draws attention to the garden trees beyond it, dissolving our separation from the natural world.

In another small setting, a grouping of magnolia branches and beloved objects create a serene corner vignette.

◊ Just as a plant seeks light no matter where it's situated, the resourceful small-apartment dweller seeks out ways to incorporate garden style. It's often the tiny details that extend our perspective and enhance the bigger themes of our lives. These elements of nature coexist gracefully with our surroundings and enable us to create a highly personal sanctuary where we can relax and thrive. ◊

Olive green walls provide an ideal backdrop for an outburst of spring color: pots of yellow and white forced daffodils, accompanied by freesia and a dendrobium orchid, are gathered on a mahogany tray set atop a small end table. They spill down a garden step-stool of weathered wood, signaling an end to winter doldrums.

Light is used as decorative sculpture in this refurbished attic retreat, where sloped ceiling angles create an arresting interplay of light and shadow on foliage and furniture. Vibrantly hued plants add flamboyant color on either side of tailored ivory divans, which are tucked into a cozy and intimate seating space. Hot-red geraniums and gerberas, set off by green striped and coated paper pots, are skillfully accented with touches of additional primary tones. Bright red apples sit in a wooden bowl, crimson pillows rest on the divans, and above this contemplative setting, an old ladder rises gracefully. Its steps double as plant stands, and the delicate shadows it throws change with the sun's position from dawn to dusk.

Resourcefully bringing the outside in is a common trait of urban garden lovers. Here a silvery teak bench creates a cozy segue from living room to deck. Pillows embroidered with insects, and a wire birdcage housing two nests add a hint of garden fauna. Eugenia, a sturdy and popular outdoor shade hedge, thrives in topiary form indoors. A large bamboo basket used as a side table holds an oncidium orchid while an exuberant spider plant spills from an antique Chinese wheat basket below. This clever garden nook opens onto a small deck, where a teak dining table is set for an alfresco lunch. Magenta carnations, procured from a corner grocery store, add a splash of color in copper tin vases and mingle with red apples in a shallow footed bowl.

37

On this dining room table, containers of red bromeliads in latte bowls evoke the colors and textures of Portugal. Light fills this exuberant, bright area, where a palette of sage, rust, gold, and burnt orange, reflected in everything from the tablecloth to the flowers, extends the rustic sun-splashed look and feel of the Mediterranean. Clusters of yellow bromeliads sit in yellow pails in a surprising rendition of a portable window box. Nearby, suspended on the wall from red organza ribbons, two additional yellow pails house trailing ivy, contributing to a look that is unconventional. Common plants and objects combine with cheerful wall paint to produce a fresh decorative approach, proving yet again that inventiveness needs only a keen eye and a bold heart.

A celadon vase with cut magnolia branches captures the theme of this tranquil bedroom: soul comfort. Set against chalk-gray walls, the futon bed, tansu chest, mementos, and plant life all combine to insure that a restful ambience prevails. Natural objects—feathers and African pods—blend effortlessly with textiles. Beside the bed, magnolia branches pruned from a nearby overhanging tree add gentle pastel colors and sensuous shapes. Understated, relaxed, and calming, the bedroom's plant and furniture choices all convey serenity, while wide windows accommodate an expansive view of the bustling city below.

Surrounded by neighboring rooftops, the deck adjacent to the bedroom of this apartment both extends the living space and creates the feeling of an urban nest. A series of tall wood-framed windows and a peek-through opening from the hallway invite in a wash of sunlight that encourages the plants grouped on a blond wood Asian trunk used as a bedside table. Night-blooming jasmine in a galvanized French flower bucket, miniature yellow roses, and violas, potted and clipped to float in a bowl, bask in the streaming sunshine.

Outside on the small balcony, there is a duplicate collection of plants and containers with the addition of flowering yellow cassia and two varieties of hebe. A chaise lounge, flattened to accommodate this plant lover's eclectic assortment, also provides seating for this garden perch.

Even a basement studio apartment in the heart of the city holds promise when viewed with a gardener's eye. A window seat is transformed to an indoor garden bench when used as a platform to display a collection of antique watering cans and ornaments. Basking in the limited sunshine, a potted purple hydrangea in a simple terra-cotta container sits on a cast concrete plinth.

An old folding garden table and chair reclaimed from a yard sale invite a quiet moment with a cup of tea and a botanical notebook. With no garden to wander in or errant weeds to pluck, at least in this setting, dreams of gardens past and future can be invoked.

45

Hot-pink primroses potted in miniature
galvanized containers line the ledges of
a sky blue tiled bathroom in this small
apartment. An easy-to-grow perennial that
is usually massed in alpine or outdoor rock
gardens, these plants become cheery and
surprising garden notes when presented
individually in a moist indoor climate.
Eventually they may make their way into
a large container on a balcony or a window
box mixed with other colorful flowering
plants. An arching, feathery potted acacia
thrives in the bathroom's humidity and low,
diffused light.

A simple cluster of gerbera daisies in an elongated green glass vase grace this marble countertop and are reflected in the mirror. Easily found in corner flower stands and supermarket floral shops, these reliable cut flowers usually have a long life, making them a good value. Here their bright fuchsia petals and yellow centers mimic the primroses' color and further enliven the scene.

THE GARDEN
Still Life

If a garden is a work of art, the gardener is an artist who paints with flowers. With a garden still life, the urban garden artist can create this art indoors. A still life offers a simple way to bring a touch of color, botanical influence, or outdoor whimsy to even the most minute corner of a city living space. In spring, you can create an arrangement of found objects such as a mossy stepping stone, an old bottle with the first camelia clipping, a diminutive gazing ball, and a treasured metal dragonfly. Fritillaria in ale glasses poised on a bird-of-paradise leaf appear completely different indoors than they would in an outdoor garden plot. In summer, an embroidered silk bag, purchased on the street in Chiang Mai, holds a cupful of common supermarket gerbera daisies superimposed against a dramatic magenta wall. In autumn, bright yellow chrysanthemums float in an amber glass boat and poke through a hole cut in a square of painted wood. Millinery trim linen flowers in a green bottle set on a rare book about native trees remind us that even in winter months, a surrogate garden icon can strike a poetic note.

As these ideas suggest, a garden still life can take as many forms as the imagination permits. In fact, in creating this kind of garden art, you are free to express your innermost garden instincts. A composition can be used to celebrate and remember moments spent in nature, or to indulge a secret adoration of a particular flower. It could also have a cherished heirloom as its focal point.

Inspired by the ever-changing seasons, a garden still life allows you to mingle memorabilia and natural elements in unusual combinations. It releases the artist in us all. In the midst of city frenzy, it stands as an altar to the serenity of the garden—a visual haiku that invites contemplation. ◖

48

C I T Y   F L A T

The style and architectural heritage of many city flats harken back to an era that was more ornate than sleek, more historical than contemporary. This old-fashioned aesthetic lends itself to a unique kind of urban heirloom garden style. Even flats designed with built-in furniture offer abundant possibilities for experimentation. Laid out in a linear fashion, with each room opening off a central corridor, the rooms in a flat often feel disconnected. Yet, like many gardens that are designed with rooms linked by a pathway, you can use this separation to your creative advantage by developing individual scenes in each. ◊ Urban flats also present an opportunity to reframe potentially awkward interiors through the fresh and enlivening perspective of the garden. You can choose to play up the building's legacy with antique garden artifacts or play against it with a contrasting modern point of view. A carved limestone fireplace, now inoperative, becomes the cozy setting for grouped pots of orchids on the mantel. Another orchid blooms next to a clear vase holding ostrich

A dendrobium orchid arches gracefully toward the light from a contemporary square mesh container. Its bright green leaves and feathery pink flowers appear more intense against the chocolate brown walls.

eggs. While these might be considered old-fashioned plants, suddenly when seen against a chocolate brown wall the room is suddenly transformed from a quiet, sedate space to a sensual, lively one. Displayed on a contemporary table in a living room, a flat of lettuce starts, replanted temporarily in a low copper bowl, adds unexpected playfulness to an austere setting and provides a visual connection to an herb garden on the deck beyond stately glass doors. ◑ Cascading ivy, azure blue ceramic pots, and brilliant orange freesia and Clivia all

An orchid gracefully arches over twin potted yellow primroses.

breathe new life into their darker, early-twentieth-century setting. Pausing to notice a reclaimed garden finial rising up from the polished wood floor near the grand piano in another urban flat, we see it as if for the first time—odd and yet familiar, out of place but perfectly in harmony with its surroundings. In the urban flat, a modern point of view mingles effortlessly with a building's history when intertwined through the gardener's eye. ◑

The intoxicating scent of a single gardenia floating in a glass cylinder vase is enough to pervade an entire room.

As if to prove that necessity is indeed the mother of invention, this unlikely, handsome dining table centerpiece resulted from one urban gardener's quick creative thinking after an unexpected downpour. This flat dweller was about to plant a mesclun lettuce mix in a large planter box on the adjoining deck when a sudden thunderstorm developed. Ever resourceful, the gardener brought the plantings inside, and lettuce starts became an inspired centerpiece. The hammered copper bowl in which the lettuce nestles resides on an industrial copper and iron table. In a day or so, when the weather clears, this same mix will be transported back outside, and dug in alongside flourishing culinary herbs. As for the copper bowl—it will await a mound of fruit—or perhaps the next rain.

Plants that need little direct light sometimes produce bright flowers, as if supplying
their own internal source of sunshine. Apricot
flowering maple, vibrant orange freesia and
Clivia, and Beedham's White Lamium—all
shade-lovers—add their vivid radiance to
this living room and alcove. Set against
a muted backdrop of wood-paneled walls,
these plants perfectly bookend two paintings on the long narrow table, picking up
colors used by the artist. In the foreground,
between a pair of dark sage velvet and
metal rolling chairs, potted Abutilon sup-
plies additional spots of color. Indirect light
filters in through the two leaded windows;
with the addition of art and multicolored
low-light plants, the spaces provides a calm
yet stimulating environment.

An older kitchen in this city flat has been updated with a flair for contemporary garden style. Ingenuity, farmers' market color, and a metal utility theme bring out the best in the brick wall and vintage O'Keefe & Merritt stove. A galvanized rack, equally at home in the potting shed, holds metallic pots of colorful plants and provides easy access to dish towels. Framed by the exposed gas pipe, two inverted graters become unexpected plant holders. Hung on hooks above the stove, they allow air to circulate and can be slipped off for watering. Red d'Anjou pears arranged gracefully on a chrome trivet create a painterly still life. Bunches of snapdragons, melon-edged yellow garden roses, and Protea will be arranged in smaller containers and distributed in other rooms. For now, they're refreshed in galvanized French flower buckets and accompanied by a bounty of citrus from the farmers' market.

Sometimes plants and flowers not only complement furnishings, but rejuvenate them, as with this floral mantelpiece. English ivy drapes from an oval gold-rimmed mirror like an elegant shawl. The abundant green foliage of this easy-to-grow indoor plant creates a satisfying contrast to the dazzling ranunculus in their curving purple glass vases, as well as to the electric white Iceland poppies. A smaller antique gold-leaf mirror has been converted into a tray that holds a potted staghorn fern, set in a gilded petal bowl.

61

Ornaments and containers inspired by the outdoors bring the variety and natural grace of a bed of perennials to this rich, flower-filled living room. A woven-branch sofa table with a wooden top extends that theme and becomes an ideal setting for an artful arrangement of purple florals. Round heads of burgundy ranunculus spill out from tinted, curved drinking glasses doing double service as vases. Two cast-concrete bowls—one filled with opened petals—squat before amethyst Cala lilies that hover above in a classic pedestal urn.

Moss collected during a trip to the country is mounded in a rustic flat wooden box that once transported tiny seedlings. Reclaimed tin finials originally used to crown a garden wall in Central America add a touch of whimsy to the elegant mix of traditional and contemporary furniture in this city flat's living room: a baby grand piano and velvet couch mingle comfortably with two bamboo, mahogany, and chrome stools and a wall of photos. Tall windows with diaphanous draperies allow warming sunlight to flood this stylish room.

Blowsy cabbage flowers from the local farmers' market burst from a hand-carved mango wood vase from Thailand. A single pink cymbidium stem curves in a free-form ceramic dish—part of an uncommon collection of plant material and containers that "floats" on top of an X-frame glass coffee table.

THE SCENT
of the Garden

While there are those who might look to air fresheners, room sprays, candles, diffusers, or incense to fragrance their home, a true garden lover wouldn't think of using anything but flowers. The scent of the garden is available to city dwellers everywhere, in any season. From heady tuberose and lilies to subtle and more delicate sweet peas and freesia, the evocative effect of a floral bouquet on our senses naturally surpasses synthetic aromas created in a laboratory. The tropical essence of a single gardenia set afloat in a small bowl of water placed on a bedside table offers a sensual greeting to stir us gently from dreams even before we open our eyes. Perhaps a single whiff of lilacs collected from the first farmers' market in spring is enough to carry us back to long-forgotten gardens and the childhood memories of lengthening days. Or maybe the redolent perfume of a bouquet of melon-colored roses, sent by a long-distance lover, stirs our heart as we turn the key in the lock at the end of a long day at work.

Making flowers a part of our daily urban lives invites the healing nature of the garden in and transforms every environment—even with the simplest approach. A single sprig of jasmine draped from a water glass on the windowsill can uplift our spirits and speak more eloquently than an extravagant arrangement displayed in an expensive container. Gathered together or individually displayed, by look and by fragrance, flowers have their own pure way of delighting our senses as they touch our hearts. ◗

L O F T

Aloft, spacious and barren, is a blank canvas awaiting the garden artist's inspiration. Its lack of definition is also its virtue—undivided floor space, high ceilings, massive windows. Most often, lofts are located in industrial—or previously industrial—neighborhoods, and their nuts-and-bolts, box-like construction may at first glance make them seem unsuited to habitation. Whether a loft serves as a live/work environment or as a dwelling, it requires daring

Delicate lilac stems, cut in staggered heights and arranged in an organically shaped stone vase, evoke memories of an old-fashioned garden with their heady scent.

and imagination to transform its drafty emptiness into warm, cozy living areas that flow comfortably from one to the next. ◗ As much as any urban dwelling, a loft offers you a chance to stretch your artistic wings and soar. Like an empty plot of land ready to be planted and cultivated, its uninterrupted expanse of wall and floor space presents a delightful opportunity to experiment: without sectional walls, plants and garden ornaments help define the dimensions of each area within the larger interior. Then, too, subtle touches of the garden can infuse a loft with warmth and color, turning it into an inviting, welcoming home. ◗ Some

loft dwellers answer the challenge of their surroundings by playfully surrendering to it. High ceilings become an asset; they allow a backyard swing to be assembled and enjoyed indoors. Unconventional lifestyles can express their unique point of view. Newsprint-clad plant containers, plant teepees transformed into singular sculptures, or a blown-up photograph printed on a linen headboard express an eclectic attitude that defies definition. Tall windows are valued for the light they bring to arrangements of plants and flowers, and the city itself becomes a backdrop that is embraced and integrated, rather than excluded or resisted. ◗ A loft, after all, is a work-in-progress, much like a painter's or sculptor's studio whose look and feel can change at a moment's whim. In the loft's open kitchen, a small living-herb pantry in summer months becomes an inviting seasonal touch. Seen through a gardener's eye, each living area benefits from even a minimal outdoor influence. This loft's dining room, formerly the elevator shaft of a wine warehouse, is graced by hand-carved stone vases filled with lilacs. ◗ Although a loft lends itself to contemporary furnishings, old-fashioned plants may look new again when met by metals and microfibers. Lofts not only are adaptable to that approach, they benefit from it as a refreshing, invigorating antidote to sterility. Free to experiment, improvise, play, and attempt the outrageous, you make

Large, square ceramic plates, exquisitely etched with an abstract leaf pattern, serve as subtle icons that remind us of nature's harmony in any setting.

your loft your home by accepting its industrial heritage and personalizing it with the garden as a partner. ◗

Although this live/work studio looks out on a busy thoroughfare, the photographer and artist who designed it insisted on emphasizing natural light. The tall windows, which open out at an angle, add a graphic element to this space. Just as the silver gelatin prints of an allee of trees shot after a hailstorm at Versailles are simply matted and framed in black, the windows frame the city views and the palm trees planted in the street divider outside.

Yellow tulips in an amber glass vase set on a folding garden table are the only accent of color, making them all the more effective. Stately juniper and baby cypress, hardy landscape plants placed indoors here, reflect the photographer's chosen subject. Newsprint secured with jute twine becomes an unexpected and smart pot cover with a new take on recycling.

73

Hand-blown antique balloon bottles, recovered from a French winery, sit like green buoys on a glass coffee table. From their narrow mouths, tall, variegated papyrus stems fan out in delicate formation. The stems' soft brown tones contrast the richness of the deep red Antherium flowers mingled among them.

Tall ceilings can dwarf a room's plants as well as its furnishings—or they can complement them. To accentuate this loft's vertical dimensions, the owner has cleverly employed two fruitwood teepees, commonly used to support climbing peas and beans in a vegetable garden. One rises up to fill a recessed cove beside the fireplace mantel, adding graphic interest to the room. The second teepee serves as a plant "frog" that anchors tall ginger flowers in a vase of English ivy. These choices exemplify the variety of options available when outdoor garden structures are reimagined for interior use. An abstract pattern on a pillow adds texture and color. Budding curly willow branches, frequently used in floral arrangements, arc up from two of three jade green vases in the fireplace beside asparagus ferns. Setting the branches in water enables them to form a root system and sprout leaves. Once the willow roots are established, the branches can be planted outside in the ground, in a large pot, or dried.

In an open urban kitchen, no matter what size, a living herbal pantry adds visual interest and puts fresh seasonings within arm's reach. Rosemary, shallots, English thyme, parsley, and bay leaves were brought in from the outside deck for the dinner about to be cooked. The bay and rosemary topiaries sit in flared unfinished wood containers placed on square wooden trays. The rough textures play well against the shiny glaze of the small brown ceramic pots that hold the other herbs. Copper plant tags pick up the metallic theme of the silver-stained wood cabinets, chrome kitchen appointments, and gleaming espresso machine on the slate countertop. Nonedible santolina, sometimes called "lavender cotton," adds its intriguing scent to the herbal mix.

pages 78–81 This chic loft is a study in urban simplicity wedded to garden fancy. With the quality of light changing as dusk slips into evening, the sweeping city views become an evolving piece of art. Hundreds of tiny green chrysanthemums create an elongated, free-form centerpiece punctuated by three heads of purple cabbage. A date palm frond is posed languorously against a corner wall for the evening. Later, after the dishes are done, the palm frond will be refreshed and displayed in a large cylinder of cool water; the mums will be gathered and set afloat with bobbing Granny Smith apples in a straight-sided round glass bowl for another playful interpretation.

Against the *tabla rosa* of this all-white room, the greens of the plants mindfully chosen as accents are intensified. Leaf shadows reflected in the single window reveal the origin of two oversized stems clipped from outdoor plantings and arranged in a tall milk-glass vase. A white ceramic bowl draped with ferny moss perches on an upended glass cylinder, an improvised plant table. Its counterpart adjacent to the vase becomes part of a contemplative still life. When seeking respite from the din and dirt of city streets, what better solution than a padded, sound-proof decompression chamber? Meditation, relaxation, reading, and garden dreaming are all appropriate activities in this tranquil setting.

Not everyone is fortunate enough to have a deck as their conference room, but this shared home office uses the adjacent outdoor space quite effectively. Leading-edge technology combines comfortably with conventional plantings. The vivid orange of the oversized table is picked up in the variegated leaves of two potted plants, cleverly reinvented here as a stepped divider to create an up-to-date partner's desk.

Out on the deck, two free-form white rocking chairs beckon the viewer to take a mid-morning coffee break in the sun. Industrial-strength container plants, the marguerites planted in stainless steel containers, bloom from spring through fall. An inverted black mesh wastebasket makes an ideal plant stand, and a metal file box that has been perforated on the bottom for drainage holds a purple hopseed bush.

A haunting sculpture of a female form
photographed at the Parisian cemetery
Pére Lachaise, enlarged and printed on
a linen headboard, becomes the focal point
of a bedroom where garden elements
mingle comfortably with books and artifacts. Eucalyptus and kumquat branches,
Kangaroo paw stems, and orange lantern
flowers form a striking composition in
metallic vases. One vase rests on a cleverly
designed pullout bookcase ladder. In the
background, a girl's ballerina dress
descends for added visual interest.

Periwinkle, Gravenstein-apple green, and
melon antique sap buckets are mounted on
a rail and hold variegated coleous leaves,
while a photograph of grass printed on a
fabric wall hanging brings another aspect
of the outdoors to this indoor room.

Continuing the fanciful theme, a child's playground swing has been mounted to the loft's high ceiling and is ready for liftoff at a moment's whim. In bold metal letters, this city dweller humorously declares her identity as a garden lover.

89

The Italianate patterns of these scroll-backed garden chairs extend the visual diversity of herbs and plants set among them. The woven wrought-iron seat of one chair is used as a stand for a blooming broom plant. Other chairs are gathered around a table displaying the exhilarating bounty of a farmstand outing—rosemary, fava bean blossoms, patty pan squash, eggplant, and lavender twigs held in miniature garden urns. Before the edibles are consumed, they lend a warm and appealing sense of natural lushness to the spare surroundings. The glass, bell-shaped cloches hark back to nineteenth-century France, where farmers used rows of them to protect tender seedlings against the elements in early spring. Technology may have advanced that process, but no one has yet devised more attractive greenhouse enclosures than the ones containing these nasturtium and baby lettuces.

91

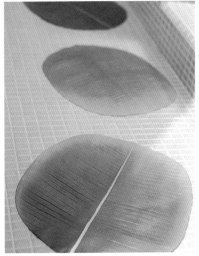

When clipped iris heads or other flowers float in small glass bowls in the bathtub as they do here, they add a decorative flourish. Brightly colored mid-twentieth-century metal drinking glasses contain iris stems, as do the low silver ceramic bowls layered with river stones and anchored with kenzu. Purple flowers contrast handsomely with the bathroom's khaki tiles, setting a festive mood.

HEALING
Houseplants

For all the effort we exert in the care and feeding of houseplants, they repay us with every breath we take. Silently vigilant, they filter out harmful pollutants from the air, convert carbon dioxide from cigarettes and other sources to oxygen, and trap dust particles. While synthetic fibers in furniture, bedding, and carpets often add durability and reduce maintenance, these same materials often release harmful chemicals.

Because plants efficient in freshening interior spaces come in a wide array of sizes, colors, and shapes, they provide sculptural versatility and add graphic greenery to any room as well. Place them strategically in carpeted areas, near computers, and anywhere with poor ventilation. You'll want to include two to three plants for every hundred square feet of living space.

Extensive research performed by NASA reveals that three specific palms are superior air fresheners—the Areca palm, the lady palm, and the bamboo palm. All three thrive in semi-sunny locations and resist pests as long as they are well watered. Also adept at filtering out contaminants are the colorful peace lilies, gerbera daisies, Boston ferns and spider plants, philodendrons, English ivy, chrysanthemum, and tulips. Cacti and succulents minimize the negative effect of computer-generated ozone.

For all their functionality, the pleasure these plants afford us cannot be measured simply in molecules. In return they require minimal care. Purifying plants need to have their leaves wiped regularly with a damp cloth to prevent the dust they collect from clogging their pores, so that they, too, can breathe freely. They prefer cooler temperatures, high humidity, and diffused sunlight. As well as contributing to our health they also provide beauty, reminding us of the leafy, verdant world beyond our four walls. ◗

INSIDE / OUTSIDE

Urban outdoor spaces come in all sizes, shapes, and locations. They may be rooftops surrounded by a wide-angle, panoramic city view or they may look out on the drainpipe of an adjacent building. Frequently, they have no garden at all, and at times they may even have been contrived by a city dweller anxious for access to air and light. In a high-rise building, there may be floor-to-floor stacks of uniform rectangular balconies with little privacy from one another and a hundred unsynchronized interpretations of plantings and furnishings. In other parts of the city, the front stoop of a building of flats may be used for neighborhood gatherings as well as a wacky assortment of plants searching for the light. The tiny balcony off a living room becomes the city version of the library, where guests so inclined can step outside for an after-dinner cigar amidst a highly personal grouping of flowering plants. ◗ Rooftops, decks, backyard gardens, terraces, balconies, landings, and fire escapes all serve the same objective for the garden-loving urban resident. They give us the space to create a

Bright leaves and flowers replicate the intense wall colors of the comfortably furnished balcony and the living room it leads to.

restorative garden setting: reconnecting our frazzled soul to a still place within. This garden setting can be achieved with only the faintest sound of water gurgling in an atrium fountain or through a lavish assortment of pots assembled over the years inside an enclosed terrace. Urban outdoor spaces lend themselves to any use or purpose demanded of them. One city house includes a terrace along the master bedroom and bath that becomes a sheltered spot to relax after a warm bath. In another city setting, a ground floor apartment opens to a tiny space that becomes a warm-weather dining room where there is none indoors. Higher up, a single step of the fire escape becomes outdoor seating for a noontime respite in the sun. ◖ All it takes is a way of seeing outdoor space as an opportunity to bring the grace the garden offers into an urban lifestyle. Improvised furniture ensembles, experimental plantings, or elegant perennial gardens all find their place in city outdoor spaces. From function to fantasy, throwing open windows and doors suggests further access to the promise a garden setting holds. Utilizing these areas allows you to create incremental space where you can escape from cramped quarters or simply extend them; you can express an impulse or cultivate your wildest dream. ◖

A cozy outdoor corner balcony becomes another room overlooking the street life below. Selected plants add further warmth to this snug perch.

Contrary to conventional wisdom, the grass isn't always greener in the other fellow's yard. This is especially true when you've created your own private city park. This imaginative grass-planted rooftop, which looks out on a pocket park below, is bordered on one side by a wall of plants in paint-box colored pots. The playful potted plant collection includes lavender, geraniums, feverfew, and santolina, all arranged with an artist's eye for composition.

Grapes, cheese, French bread, and a bottle of wine are set out on a blanket, spread near a volunteer purple anemone shooting up through the grass. Inside, wooden benches continue the verdant theme with moss-colored upholstered seats arranged under a curtain-draped skylight. Potted lemon trees, an antique green watering can, and aluminum furniture complete this enchanting urban version of *Dejeuner sur l'Herbe*.

pages 102–105 With a splendid city sky-line as its backdrop, this atrium greenhouse combines quirky garden ornaments with indoor-outdoor furnishings and flowers. Textures, fabrics, colors, and architectural materials inventively mix and mingle. Covering the terrazzo tile floor are three hassocks, a Chinese lacquered stool, and a collection of potted plants. Tasseled Fortuny lamps provide pockets of light, and bamboo shades filter out glare from the cityscape window. Close by, a cherubic garden angel's hands fondle strings of green beads. Plants and flowers are present in profusion and include pieris in terra-cotta pots, yellow cymbidium orchids, oncidium orchids, nocturnally fragrant nicotiana, ferns, palms, and lichen-covered tree branches where delicate butterfly specimens alight.

105

This secret garden is tucked into a small outdoor space adjacent to a ground floor apartment. Crammed with shade-loving plants that produce an early bloom, it will evolve throughout the coming seasons. Now, it challenges the visitor to look closely for climbing jasmine blossoms about to burst open, and trailing fuchsia, candy tuft, Cala lilies, and impatiens show off their newly opened flowers. Rose-colored fairy primrose is nicely complemented by a square blue container set on a salmon tablecloth.

Savvy urbanites with a garden perspective recognize any opportunity to create creature comforts. While fire escapes are typically meant for little more than a last-ditch exit strategy, they offer imaginative possibilities to the enterprising apartment dweller. Here, a kitchen chair cushion sits on one stair, creating a unique spot to catch some rays of the midday sun amidst potted geraniums, feverfew, and native grass, as well as colorful hand-blown glass balls in terra-cotta containers. All are strikingly set against a scene of industrial buildings, billboards, and live/work spaces.

Cityscape and rooftop views provide a dramatic backdrop to this rear apartment deck. Its Moorish windscreen cutouts enhance the North African theme established by its Moroccan blue walls and ceiling. Desert succulents in white and pastel pots boldly stand out against the vibrant pigment wash. An eclectic selection of pots ranging from pottery shards embedded in concrete to seashell-encrusted ceramics add their own interest. An old chimney pipe is stationed on the weathered teak table and holds a bouquet of protea, flax leaves, bear grass, and dianthus. A protected haven on the one hand, yet designed to be open to the buzz of nearby urban activity, the deck's cheerful colors counter the stresses of the workday.

Rooftop access through the living-room door opens this flat to a panoramic view and an opportunity for a garden-party setting. Set for a new interpretation of cocktails at seven, vintage awning-striped camp chairs and glowing orange paper lanterns add their vibrant accents as the sun sets and the city lights twinkle on. Candytuft, pale yellow primroses and flax are planted in contemporary triangulated zinc containers in this urban garden.

This festive communal rooftop setting instantly conjures up chips, salsa, and mariachi music. Perched above urban live/workspace lofts in a converted industrial building, the weathered dining table is a centerpiece for an assortment of French bistro chairs, a galvanized plant container used as a seat, and a garden step stool. Bright striped cushions unify the seating arrangement and coordinate with the intense colors of the flowers. To add even more dazzle, fiery orange and hot-pink ribbed pots are used as containers. Note the human figure carved into one leg of the gracefully sagging table; think of him as the garden sage who sees all and never tells tales.

Outdoor urban spaces sometimes turn up in quirky locations. This small balcony sits outside a bathroom. What to do? Reconfigure the two areas as one mini-spa, with a place to relax post bath. To create a sense of flow between indoors and out, galvanized metal is used in both areas for furniture and plant holders. Reblooming Christmas cacti, an excellent choice inside, add dollops of green and magenta to enliven the monochromatic white bathroom. Its slate floor opens onto the balcony, where a terrarium sits on stones in a galvanized tray. The overall effect is to tie the bathroom and balcony together as a private sanctuary for warm-weather use.

Rooftops will always be the great escape for harried urban dwellers. Stretched out in a yellow Adirondack chair, you can catch the last rays of the sun as the city falls away below. The clean, stark, monochromatic lines of an elevator structure and the gravel floor are punctuated by cheerful blue, yellow, and aqua Gladding, McBean vases. Like heirloom plants, their pottery molds have been handed down unchanged. Just across the roof deck, a row of dried bamboo stalks creates a curtain-like sculpture when sunk into a low slate bench. In all, with minimal furnishings, decoration, and plant materials, this rooftop becomes an ideal place for repose and reflection at the end of the day.

RESOURCE
Guide

Aria
1522 Grant Street
San Francisco, CA 94133
415.433.0219
Obscure French and American
objects from the 19th century
on. Industrial lighting and
furniture oddities.

Arkitektura In-Situ
560 Ninth Street
San Francisco, CA 94103
800.400.4869
and
474 North Old Woodward Avenue
Birmingham MI 48009
800.844.1126
Contemporary furniture, kitchen, and
bath for the cooler establishment.

Atelier 142 Gallery
2354 Market Street, Suite #2
San Francisco, CA 94114
415.861.8216
James Scott Garas and painter
Daniel Tousignant: fine photography
and paintings of things natural and
beautiful are showcased in this light-
filled gallery.

Bluestone Main
120 Petaluma Boulevard North
Petaluma, CA 94954
707.765.2024
A wonderful collection of colorful,
garden-inspired goods for interior
and exterior spaces.

Cliff's Hardware and Home
479 Castro Street
San Francisco, CA 94114
415.531.5368
Like an old five-and-dime with
everything one would need to fulfill
creative endeavors.

Crate & Barrel
Stores nationwide and catalog
800.323.5461
Vases, containers, furniture, and
more with contemporary style and
diversity.

Design Within Reach
455 Jackson Street
San Francisco, CA 94111
Catalog: 800.944.2233
Chic and stylish furniture, lighting of
modern consciousness.

Floorcraft Garden Center
550 Bayshore Boulevard
San Francisco, CA 94124
415.824.1900
Herbs, shade-loving plants, twig fenc-
ing, trellises, and wise plants-people.

The Gardener
1836 Fourth Street
Berkeley, CA 94710
510.548.4545
Never lacking in soulful home accou-
trements and hand-rendered goods.
This store is always a treat for those
with an appreciation for inspired
objects.

Gardeners' Eden
Stores and catalog
800.822.1214
Elegant garden furniture, dinnerware
and plants (such as miniature grow-
ing pineapple).

George
2411 California Street
San Francisco, CA 94115
415.441.0564
and
1829 Fourth Street
Berkeley, CA 94710
510.644.1033
Picky people still have pets. Where to
shop for Fido and Fifi when you
won't compromise for less than
perfect beds, bowls, and pet snacks.

Helie Robertson
for Gladding, McBean Pottery
415.757.7083
The contact for the spicy-colored
architectural ceramic glazed urns
and garden pots.

Ikea
Stores nationwide
800.434.4532
Efficient, affordable, resourceful
design. Galvanized containers, vases,
ceramic pots. Endless.

Illuminations
Stores nationwide and catalog
800.226.3537
Candles, accessories, and table tops
from bronze to glass for glowing
interiors.

Intérieur Perdue
340 Bryant Street
San Francisco, CA 94107
415.543.1616
Rural French garden antiques and
curiosities. Furniture, ornament, and
linens, all directly imported and bril-
liantly inspired.

Jamson Whyte
1345 Howard Street
San Francisco, CA 94103
415.355.1345
Natural home furnishings from
southeast Asia, rendered in rich teak
with original, clean design.

Limn
290 Townsend Street
San Francisco, CA 94107
415.543.5466
and
501 Arden Way
Sacramento, CA 95815
916.564.2900
An exemplary, complete selection of
the best modern design. Silverware
to sofas, lighting to vanities.

The Magazine
1823 Eastshore
Berkeley, CA 94710
510.549.2282
and
528 Folsom Street
San Francisco, CA 94105
415.777.4707
Interior and garden furniture culled
from the best of modern design.

Museum of Modern Art
New York
Store and catalog
800.447.6662
From grassy picnic mats to paper
vases. Techy and sensual, early and
contemporary design.

Nest Egg
550 San Anselmo Avenue
San Anselmo, CA 94960
415.455.0581
Rustic and playful items for the
home reminiscent of country
gardens. The owner handmakes
one-of-a-kind, tiny bird nests.

Ohmega Salvage
2407 San Pablo Avenue
Berkeley, CA 94702
510.843.7368
Top quality architectural salvage.
Knobs, windows, ironwork, and
ornament flourishes.

Paxton Gate
824 Valencia Street
San Francisco, CA 94110
415.824.1872
The oddest garden store of all.
Glass orbs in astronomical colors,
tillandsias, Japanese tools—all
with a appreciation for less obvious
natural beauty.

Plastica
8405 W. Third Street
Los Angeles, CA 90048
323.655.1051
Sassy accessories and gifts, virtually
all rendered in plastic (or some
variation on the theme), notably
including wood-look bolster pillows.

Rayon Vert
3187 Sixteenth Street
San Francisco, CA 94103
415.861.3516
Vases, lighting, gorgeous flowers,
and select plants.

Restoration Hardware
Stores and catalog
800.762.1005
Witty and well-resourced home goods
and furniture, covering the whole
home with style.

Smith & Hawken
Stores nationwide and catalog
800.776.3336
The venerable source for tasteful
garden goods. Furniture that lasts
and looks good.

Star Antiques and Collectibles
1415 Valencia Street
San Francisco, CA 94109
415.289.9939
An eclectic collection for urban
spaces large and small.

Sue Fisher King
3067 Sacramento Street
San Francisco, CA 94115
415.922.7276
and at Wilkes Bashford
375 Sutter Street
San Francisco, CA 94108
415.398.2894
Linens, bath, and tableware (including
luscious Christian Tortu lettuce
plates) of the utmost taste.

Yardart
2188 Sutter Street
San Francisco, CA 94115
415.346.6002
Timeless antique garden ornament
and furniture, both large and
small scale.

Zonal
1942 Fillmore Street
San Francisco, CA 94115
415.359.9111
and over four other Bay Area stores.
Purveyor of seating, storage, and
slumber-oriented furnishings. Rusty
to rich.

Special Credits

We wish to mention some of the
architects, artists, builders, designers,
and sources that helped to create the
stunning spaces in which we did our
photography.

cover
Interior courtesy of Pamela Fritz,
Interieur Perdue. Chairs and bowl:
The Magazine, San Francisco, CA.
Zinc Planters: Smith & Hawken, San
Francisco, CA.

pages 46, 47, 78, 79, 80-85
Kate and Shane Ginsberg credit
the following:
Architect: Nilus De Matran,
San Franciso, CA.
Dining room table: Elizabeth Page
Smith designed, from Jenny Armit
Design, Los Angeles, CA.
Dining room chairs: by Capellini
(Jasper Morrison).
White room was Shane's own design
concept.
Bathroom/Kitchen cabinetry:
George Slack Cabinet Maker,
San Francisco, CA.

pages 34-37, 40, 41
John Sellwood and Rick Rankin
thank each other for design, building,
and remodeling.

pages 88-101, 107-109
Deborah Bishop and Michael
Liberman credit:
Architect, Alan Rudy, San
Francisco, CA.
Erik Dreher for horticulture and
painted pots, San Francisco, CA.

pages 72, 73
James Scott Garas, artist and
photographer, represented at Atelier
142 gallery, San Francisco, CA.

pages 10-21, 24, 25,
Sandra Slater credits:
Architect: Esherick, Homsey,
Dodge & Davis, San Francisco, CA.
General Contractor: Drew Maran
Construction, Palo Alto, CA.
Water Sculpture: Futon Cheng,
Berkeley, CA.

pages 54-57, 76, 77, 92, 93
Dr. Dan Siedler credits:
Architect: Daren Joy, of
North American Stijl Life,
San Francisco, CA.

*pages, 68-70, 86, 87, 102,-105, 112, 113,
116, 117*
Wendy Earl credits:
Jeffery Pilotte Design for dining
table, bamboo outdoor sculpture,
cabinetry, San Francisco, CA.
Elena Dorfman, photographer of
headstone for Wendy Earl's
bed-backboard concept.

*pages 22, 23, 44, 45, 74, 75, 90, 91,
114, 115*
Jacqueline Bass and Dr. Stephen
Walrod credit:
Moore, Ruble, and Yudell Architects,
Santa Monica, CA.

pages, 64, 65
David Salinitro credits:
Photographer Todd Hido, represented
by Stephen Wirtz Gallery,
San Francisco, CA.